TRAYVON B. MARTIN
HIS LAST VISIT TO SANFORD

LEOPOLD   PRYCE

All rights reserved
Copyright © 2013 L. Pryce

DEDICATION

His death was not in vain, it was not a lost cause; it has brought life back to a people who were dead to the facts that black people do not get treated equally under the law. There is great revival breaking forth that black lives matter.

There is a great awakening right across America and the world they have now seen the light…love is greater than hate and peace transcends the boundaries of war.

Your name will not soon be forgotten: Trayvon B. Martin; rest awhile.

Acknowledgements

Thanks to all of you who have contributed to this book: you took time out of your busy schedules to look at my work and made corrections. Without your encouragements and your constant asking: 'what happened to your book…man? I would not be able to move forward with it; thanks again.

TRAYVON B. MARTIN HIS LAST VISIT TO SANFORD

Heinous, Tragic, and heart breaking are just a few of the words one can use to describe the Trayvon Martin saga. Where to begin honestly, it is hard to tell, what to make of the situation; was it just a matter of racism or just plain lets make on example of this out- of- place black boy walking through a community which I am protecting, The accused, George may have considered but on the surface, he did not show any racist behaviour towards blacks, according to his family and friends.

Over the course of this trial; many people have voiced their opinions on all the possible scenarios of what police reports have said took place that night.

Everyone was dumb-founded when they learned details of Florida's STAND–YOUR-GROUND LAW which basically says: if you are a licensed gun owner, you can legally shoot to kill the other person whom you might think is a threat to you. What is most frightening is, one does not have to see a weapon on the other person to pull the trigger. The only report you need to relay to the authorities is that you were in fear of you life, and that is enough to get you complete protection against any criminal charges.

What many were beginning to understand is that there was no single factor that one could point to as a motivator in the death of this young man, there are multiple factors like: racism, the **STAND YOUR GROUND LAW**, rage, anger,(on both sides), distrust, etc. Based on the facts that are public knowledge; many people have said that they are willing to say that George is solely responsible for his actions against Trayvon, on that cold February night. We know that he was the one who pulled the trigger, he did confessed to that but what made him do it? That is the question many are asking.

Did the STAND YOUR GROUND Law give strength to George to pull the trigger knowing full well that he could be acquitted of all charges? Supporters were asking …all he had to remember is the STAND-YOUR-GROUND law which says: if you reasonably believe that you face imminent death, serious bodily injury, rape, kidnapping, or (in most states)robbery, you can use deadly force against the assailant, even if you have a perfectly safe avenue of retreat.

Supporters were now beginning to understand that this case was not just about the accused man's action which took place on that cold February night, it also: had much to do with Florida's stand your ground law. On the 12th day into the deliberation; supporters of Trayvon Martin were truly beginning to understand the complexity of the case. Maybe Trayvon was there sitting down beside his God, saying; I wish I could go back and tell them, don't even bother to fight for me; it's a lost cause because the law is not on our side…

Whatever the outcome is; there is going to be overwhelming grief on one side and euphoria on the other. But who is the winner in all of this? No one, absolutely, no one! Supporters were saying loud and clear.

GEORGE'S BACKGROUNG…

George. was born on October 5th, 1983 in Manassas, Virginia. He is the 3rd of 4 children, one brother two sisters. His mother was born in Peru and has some black Ancestry, through her Afro-Peruvian maternal grandfather. His father is an American of German descent. His father served 22 years in the military working for the Department of Defence for the last 10 years. He also worked as a magistrate in Fairfax County's 19th Judicial District.

George had identified himself as Hispanic on voters registration forms.

George was raised as Catholic and served as an altar boy from age 7-17.

At age 14, George joined an after-school Junior Reserve Officers' Training Corps program because he wanted to become a Marine. After graduating high school, George moved to Lake Maria, Florida where he got a job at a Insurance Agency. He took classes at nights to obtain a license to sell Insurance. According to friends of George, in 2004, he and an Afro-American friend opened a satellite office of Allstate Insurance which eventually failed a year later.

In 2007, newly married George and his wife moved to a Retreat at Twin Lakes in Sanford, they rented a townhouse there. He enrolled in a Seminole State College, 2009 and was working on his associate degree in Criminal Justice. Even though he was (a course credit) shy of his degree, he was allowed to participate in a school graduation ceremony, in December 2011. At the time of the shooting, George was working on completing that credit. He was also employed as an insurance underwriter during that period.

In early 2011, George was a witness to the beating of a homeless man by the son of a white Sanford police officer. He was among the protesters who were gathered at the Sanford City Hall. During the meeting, George claimed that he witnessed disgusting behaviour while he was in a ride-along program with local police. However; the Police Department said that it cannot recall the accused being part of that program.

From the little that is now known about George; he doesn't appear to be one who was a trouble maker or racist in the past. He seemed to have had good upbringing. he really appeared to be a man who was constantly looking for new ways to improved his life.

Could it be that George felt stifled by the fact that nothing was really working out in his favour, after trying his hands at a few things, some have asked. His social life wasn't on track either, according to reports.

Did he reach his breaking point? Some people believe that he was a very frustrated man but could that have pushed him over the edge to commit such unforgivable act? With that said; the public is beginning to wonder how could a seemingly level-headed - man, finds himself embroiled in a murder case such as this (Trayvon B. Martin's)? Was the law to be blamed for that? Did the law fail both the accused and Trayvon? that is what supporters want to know.

GOD IS IN THIS...
WHAT REALLY HAPPENED?

Now that I have taken that brief look at George's background, it is equally important that I also look at Trevor's background and ask these burning questions, How did we manage to get here? Or maybe the question should be: how did this Trayvon Martin saga got to this point? Well, here are some facts about Trayvon:
This Afro-American kid, Trayvon B. Martin; born February 5, 1995, lived with his mother in Miami Gardens, Florida. Trayvon had one older brother whom he admired very much. He wanted to go to College like his big brother did. He was very ambitious, said his brother. He loved sports. He loved to smile. No one could stay sad around Trayvon because of is infectious smiles and warmth.

In Feb, 2012, Trayvon was visiting his father, Tracy Martin, who lives in Sanford, Florida. The reason for his visit during this time of year is not in question. However let's say he had some time on - hands after he had received a 10-day suspension from his Senior High School.

Regardless of the reason for the suspension, he was in Sanford to spend time with his dad.

I was a young man too; I know very well what it is like to get away from your regular place of residence and going to spend time in a new place among families and friends, you may not have not see for awhile. It refreshes the brain. Makes one feels alive and important.

Trayvon had just received a ten day suspension from his Senior High School. I have no doubt that he had just wanted to get away from that situation and all the other stuff that teenagers battle on a daily basis. He was a young man trying to find himself.

The decision to visit his father must have been a very exciting moment. I know that I would have been totally excited. I would be thinking about how we are going to hang out as father and son…man to man and maybe talk some man-to-man stuff but what Trayvon didn't know as he visited his father was that it would have been his last visit to Sanford.

It was alleged that Trayvon did struggle with disciplinary issues, during his high school years. He was suspended 3 times during his junior year for tardiness, possession of drug paraphernalia and vandalism; if all that is true, it would be nothing new in regards to teenagers…that is what teenage kids do, they sample new ideas.

There is no doubt that most of us have been through the evolution of teenage years. Some fell through the cracks of the system and never made good of their lives; most, however, have evolved into decent human beings, preparing the way for their own families and thus the challenges starts afresh.

With that said; Trayvon was never charged with a crime and he had no juvenile record, despite those infractions in his life.

TRAGIC EVENING

Facts: Trayvon had gone to the store and picked up Skittles and a can of ice tea.
One can see that he was just being a kid having his hands occupied with the goodies he had just bought, and the good thing is that he was not at the store to buy booze or cigarettes with the intention of going off to hang out with some gang members.

He did not shop lift anything from the store and being chased by the cops like some kids his age. He bought his stuff and left the store like the son every parent would like to have.

As a 17 year old boy, walking away from the store heading to my dad's place, I know what I would be thinking but the story is not about me, it's about Trayvon. Maybe at this point; he was thinking bout his mom hoping she was fine but at the same time very happy to be away for a while being with his dad. Maybe he was smiling to himself how he is gonna rush home and hug his dad, something they may not have done in a while.

He had something to munch on; Skittles and drink. I can see him now, cant wait to get back home to take in a game of basket ball but that did not happen, instead; his life was brutally taken away.. At this point, only knows the accused knows why he had to shoot Trayvon, and the big question here is why did he shoot to kill? Of course, we might never know for sure. Did he plan in his heart to teach black kids a lesson? Was Trayvon the sacrificial lamb? Had God prepared him for a greater mission? Alternatively, maybe here, I am just grasping at straws.

In all of this… well, let us be honest, there were reports of homes in that area which were broken into by young black men. Trayvon, was shot not long after those reports. Had the accused, been pushed over the edge by personal issues to commit such a deadly ACT because of the reported break-ins? We may never know.

Allow me to ask this question, did the accused, already made up in his mind to shoot a black kid … any black kid? Does that mean Trayvon was at the wrong place at the wrong time? Another black kid is now part of the statistic of endangered species.

This is a very sad time to be a part of the human family because there are so many other humans out there who are not thinking like rational human beings… they are mad!

So the accused man said he shot the kid because he had to defend himself. At that point, maybe he didn't intentionally shoot to kill Trayvon but something went terribly wrong and he had to lie to cover his tracks. Lets give the accused the benefit of the doubt here: Something happened that night, we don't know how it happened. So let us not rush to any tentative judgment here that he shot the kid because he was black and was wearing a hoodie.

LOOK AT IT THIS WAY…

This is a very scary situation… if this was a deliberate shoot to kill; then none of us is safe. Because the accused man when out of his way to confront Trayvon then shot him through the heart and after all the death and mayhem; he sought to use the stand your ground law as his defense.

It could have been any black person walking home from the store that rainy night, with hoodie on his/her head and whose life would have suddenly snuffed out by an overzealous night watchman; this is very scary indeed!
No one reported any suspicious activities that evening. There were no suspicious persons being chased that night that one would be lead to say that there is a suspicious person in the area.

Trayvon did not know that it would have turned out to be that he was at the wrong place at the wrong time… The young man was just walking home care free with Skittles and Ice tea in hand.

Some people have suggested that the accused, has an evil heart or he had some evil intentions boiling up inside his heart for a while why he had to lie about Trayvon being a suspect and he then pursued him to fulfill his evil desire.

At this point, not much has been said about Trayvon being on the phone with his girl friend, telling her that he had been followed and feared it could be a sexual predator. The evening was getting dark, so what would one expect an unarmed teenager to do…, if I was that teenager, I know what I would have done: run like a tiger to my dad's place.

According to reports of his chat with his girlfriend, Trayvon said 'he had been followed,' simple means that he was heading home.

TRAYVON'S LAST MOMENTS

What really took place in those last moments of Trayvon's life, we can only stand by and imagine. We don't know if he had called for his mother or his father. We don't know if he had looked George in his eyes and said, please don't kill me! We don't know if he cried any tears and if he did, were those tears flowing like rivers down his cheeks.

On that cold February night, did Trayvon ask why me God, why me? Why did I have to meet upon this person tonight? And if he did ask those questions did he get an answer and if he did get an answer, did he reply…? Did he get enough time to reply?

As far as I know Trayvon came from a Christian family background, maybe before he took his last breath he had asked God to forgive his killer, wouldn't that be just great. That would have shown his strength and humility.

George was told more than once not to follow the person he called, "a suspicious person," but he chose to disregard the dispatcher's directives and continued to pursue the person he knew nothing about.

The accused said, "he drove past Trayvon near his friend's house and stopped near the Club House" (it is only a few minutes from where he said he drove pass Trayvon). He continued to say, 'Trayvon walked back to where he had parked his truck to a short distance from where the vehicle was parked; then came back and circled his vehicle while he was still sitting in it.'

Wait a minute; does that make any sense? one bystander asked. Put yourselves in Trayvon's shoes: he did not have a knife or a gun in his possession; what is the chance of him wanting to pick a fight in the dark with a stranger? He was not the one taking Martial Art's lessons…he continued.

On the other side of the argument, some people are saying that teenagers are unpredictable… Trayvon may have started the fight for any number of reasons. Other have said that they cannot see what could have motivated Trayvon to pick a fight with a stranger in the dark when all he had in his position was a package of Skittles and a canned drink.. when in fact; his original plan was to heading home to watch a Basketball game which was on TV.

Here is the thing that most people are looking at; the young man is fresh out of high school; he had left all his troubles behind looking to have some relaxing moments with his dad; he wasn't looking for trouble. The last thing that kid would want to do is to disappoint his dad.

Some people have suggested that the crime might have been committed before the 911 call took place because the accused man had a lot of time on his hand in the dark to shoot the teenager in the heart and then set the perfect scene for the police to come see.

Well maybe not so perfect a – scene because a lot of untruths were discovered in the accused stories, according to official reports by the Police Department.

From what I have observed; it would seem that The accused had a lot of powers in high places on his side, and I DON'T MEAN 'VOODOO' powers! His defense team was able to get the jury to look away from the possibilities that he could have killed the teenager within those four minutes which the defense claimed Trayvon could have ran home.

WALK WITH ME..

Walk with me down memory lane here. Moments after the 911 call, it was reported that a gunshot was heard in the area. Now think seriously here; it was not 5 or 10 minutes later, it was only moments! One does not have to be a genius to know what happened in those moments: there were very minor injuries to one and death to the other.

Here is your Chance America, to look at this tragedy through honest lenses. No! let me take that back. You don't need lenses; you don't need 20/20 vision, just your regular vision will do and, if you are blind, even that isn't an excuse for you not to see that this picture that the accused man has painted of the crime scene does not make sense but still I am willing to keep an open mind throughout…

HERE IS THE SITUATION-

Here is the situation: the accused man got out of his SUV, he was told not to pursue the person he called a suspect and, that he should get back to his truck. He disobeyed the directives of the dispatcher and did his own thing.

If you are honest readers or observers: you will see that I am not being biased in laying out the facts of this case. I have listened to both sides of this case and I have come to one conclusion; Trayvon did not have to die especially with a bullet to the heart.

Trayvon's death is what most people around the Globe are talking 'bout right now and the only word they can find to describe his death is (EVIL). The devil from hell appeared in the form of a human person, and he did destroy another innocent life and he disrupted another family's way – of – life and way of thinking. That, my friends, is the evil side of man, which makes the world less enticing.

...**STRIKES AGAINST THE ACCUSED**

OK so, be honest with yourselves here, how many strikes can you list against the accused up to this point? I have listed 7 strikes of my own below.

1. He got out of his SUV.
2. He was told not to pursue the person.
3. He was told to get back to his truck.
4. He pursued TRAYVON.
5. He had a loaded gun.
6. He confronted an unarmed teenager.
7. He shot and killed the UNARMED teenager.

There is a long list of strikes against the accused but those are the major ones, I believe, that led up to TRAYVON'S death.

THE FIGHT, WHO STARTED IT?

Before I write anything about the fight (and if there was any...) and who might have started it: lets back-up a little bit here and ask ourselves THE big question, does race have anything to do with this tragedy? Keep in mind that one of the accused man's relatives wanted to testify that he had made racial remarks against blacks in the past (that evidence was not allowed for the prosecution to present to the court). I don't think anyone is saying for sure that the accused man felt the same way about blacks when he pursued Trayvon. Well we might never know but there are allegations by people who know the family that The accused and his family are proud racists. I cannot say for sure, because I don't know the family and I was not there... to hear their alleged racist remarks for myself but that aside; let's look at his words in action that cold and wet February night...

"Those f—ing punks always get away."
"Those a—holes."
Did his words speak volumes to how he might have felt about black people before the death of Trayvon? Was he experiencing some sort of nervous break down? Was he on drugs?

OK, let us be fair. All of us have experienced some bad days on the job. Some of us are able to handle bad situations better than the other person can, but that does not give anyone the right to take another person's life, under no situation.

It does not matter what situation the accused was faced with; he had no right to pursue Trayvon and then for some unknown reasons, he shot him through the heart. and right at this moment as I am writing, it does appear that THE ACCUSED MAN will get away with the death of Trayvon B. Martin. Another innocent life wasted…, wasted!

To make matters worst; there were a number of youths who came forward to report having being harassed by the accused in the past but the court did not want anything to do with those supporting testimonies for Trayvon… they were never heard.

TALKING POINTS

I sat there in my living room listening to the media, trying to make sense of the talking points of some of the analysts: lawyers, prosecutors, former prosecutors, etc. I was bewildered by some of the things I heard coming from their mouths, things like: …Trayvon jumped from behind the bushes and sucker – punched The accused (that's believable)? Another lame point I heard was…

'There is no doubt that Trayvon was on top beating the crap out of the accused, bashing his head over- and over again on the side walk(because The accused is soft, no muscles and he is over-weight)'.

You poor thing – 200 pound man who had some training in Martial Arts; getting beat up badly by a 150 pound kid who never had any training in Martial Arts and he was never in the GYM lifting weights to built on his natural- God – given strength. Dear GOD! Get a hold of yourselves experts! Think before you talk!

Another area of total disgust was the fact that the TV analysts have now made Trayvon out to be the aggressor. Trayvon was now the "trouble maker", they have concluded. According to them; he assaulted that nice neighborhood watchman and if he was alive he could have been charged and likely do time for that assault. Here is what some people are asking: Trayvon didn't know his killer; he didn't know the neighborhood; would he really have had the guts to pick a fight? Or would he be foolish enough to want to pick a fight? is also a fair question to ask.

The opinions of most people I came across here is that the analytical views, leading up to the trail were most troubling.

From my area of observation; I could also see that it wasn't just the TV analysts who were trampling all over Travyon's rights; it was also this STAND-YOUR-GROUND law which exist in the State of Florida among other States.. That law has made a very clear statement which says that, person 'A' can shoot person 'B' dead and not much will come of it if person 'A' can prove that person 'B' poses a threat; that is incredible….some people might say frightening, to them it is frightening.

May I say here, that while I was writing this book; the Jurors had rendered their verdict and as the world is watching and hoping for justice; people all over the world are in awe. The system has failed another black young man. Right at this moment, people can't help but to be in tears, young and old. Some are speechless, incredulous, dismayed in the verdict. Is there any fairness in the law? People are asking. Is there any justice in the system for black and brown citizens? When will this unfairness ends? people are asking.

What can I say. The Jurors have spoken. They have made their decision. They have spoken from their hearts; their voices echoed around the GLOBE loud and clear. We now know that they we unable to find Trayvon's killer guilty of murder.
Justice may not have prevailed for Trayvon and his family in the manner we all wanted but I don't think his death was in vain. Blacks and other people for justice are protesting more frequently now than ever before with one voice, when the ugly face of injustice shows its face.

    I have seen a great change coming where police officers will have to be more accountable for their actions in regards to abusing black men and women then try to cover it up. Cases like that in New York, where a black man who was un-armed was choked to death by a police officer; it was captured on video, there was no chance to sweep that under the rug.

    In Ferguson: a young, 18 year old un-armed black man was gun down by a white police officer, it couldn't be covered up because there were witnesses and some video evidences in support of the victim.

    In Baltimore a young black man died in police custody. The citizens protested with one voice and the authorities heard.

In Cleveland; a police officer had found it necessary to stand on the hood of a car driven by a black person and he emptied his gun (or just about…) in the driver and a passenger who was sitting in the front seat. It was not because the occupants of the car was shooting back why he did what he did, but the officers involved thought they had heard gun fire coming from the vehicle, when it was just the muffler back fired. That is shocking. The officer assuredly was indicted because of public pressure but was soon set free later because of technicalities (something like…he thought his life was in eminent danger). Yes, I understand; many of those officers involved may not be serving time behind bars at this time but the tide is turning in the way police officers abuse young black men then try to cover it up. No longer can they chase down a black man (like what happened in Carolina, April, 2015) and shot him in the back and don't expect that some one somewhere is going to capture that on video.

There is a greater demand for transparency than ever before and that is a good thing. If police officers can't trust themselves to serve and protect in a justifiable manner then they will have to wear body cameras. Every corner of the country, people are demanding that officers be required to wear those cameras. That is why I have said, God is in this. All is not lost in this Trayvon Martin's case. The whole Country is saying enough is enough!

FOUND NOT GUILTY

The accused was found not guilty in spite of the fact that he told the entire world that he was responsible for Trayvon's death and, he had no coherent explanation why he shot the kid through the heart 'till he was dead. He was not found guilty, even after he stumbled all over his own versions of what took place that night. He smiled and walked away when he heard the authoritative voice of the law said; you were not at fault because Trayvon confronted you and you had all right to defend yourself against that unarmed teenager. Oh, well, that is the system, right or wrong; that is the system.

You are now free to go, the accused heard. Those famous words echoed under the bright lights on that sad evening. I meant, really, really sad evening for millions around the Globe who did not even know Trayvon or his family. It was not an easy verdict for anyone to listen to. Is there no moral guide lines which can act as a governing body for this legal system? Is this system so weak that it puts people lives at risk all the days of their lives because they are not sure if their neighbors will shoot to kill over any silly little argument that could spring up out of no- where.

In this age of advancement rationality; no one (out side of this STAND-YOUR-GROUND LAW Jurisdiction) was expecting to see the accused walked free after he had confessed to Trayvon's murder. For many it was very difficult to digest… very difficult to comprehend.
People everywhere are saying that Trayvon was murdered for the second time and this time it was by a system that was supposed to have had his back. Even in death; he was deserving of a fair trial, but it would appeared that the system failed him miserably.

CAN WE ALL JUST GET ALONG.

Thinking back now; I do recall one member of the defense team did say that, had Trayvon survived the shot, he most likely would have been charged with assaulting the accused man. It might not sound realistic to many of you but trust me; the lawyer for the defense was not smiling when he spoke those words; he was dead serious.

In this era of enlightenment and civility, one would think that such injustice towards any one group of people would have been eradicated by now.

Looking back at human history, we see that nations broke apart in all phases of advancement when their citizens had to endure injustice and unfair practices by the governing bodies.

Those in power need to realize that unjust laws will not advance a nation; they do not bring about lasting peace and prosperity. It is time for change, people... meaningful change.

... PUNCHED IN THE FACE?

Listen, with all the death, destruction and injustices that have surrounded this case, I am still willing to give the accused the benefit of the doubt, that he was sucker-punched in the face and fell to the ground.
After he fell, let's say he lost consciousness for a bit. When he regained his senses he realized that Trayvon was on top of him punching his face 20 times and bashing his head more than 20 times on the concrete.

Ok, stop. Hold your Horses there Mr. your stories are twisting and turning....

If anyone believes that a human being could have received 20 bare- knuckled punches to the face and 20 bashings of the head on a concrete pathway and suffered no broken bones, forget about it; it is not possible, said a protester

In addition to that, he got up and walked away, in his right mind, having just some minor scratches on his head and a so-called broken nose that was corrected within 4 hours… after all that beating?

People who care about the truth have said, No to your stories, no to what sounds your lies! Man-up and take ownership for the crime you have committed. The death of Trayvon is a great evil that was committed under the heavens and it will not be soon forgotten.

Did you see any swelling on the accused face? I did not see any. There was no swelling on the sides or the back of his head. He had no swollen lips, nothing! There should have been significant swelling in his facial area after all that beating he said he received at the hand of the unarmed teenager.

One observer said, as I sat there in his living room and listened to the accused description of how he was beaten and how he had been man-handled by this 17 year old boy; he really was not impressed because he did not look like a man who was beaten and traumatized only hours before.
He looked fit--- a man ready to do his regular duties. He told authorities the next day that he was feeling well enough to go back to work immediately; what does that say about his account of the event he is now relaying to authorities.

I looked at the police video of the accused the next day and I exclaimed; they've got the wrong man! Is that not the same guy who has claimed he was beaten up badly by Trayvon? I waited for answers but everyone around me was dumbfounded.

Here is what I expected to see on a person who had just got beaten up as the accused had described:
- Broken scalp
- Concussion
- Bleeding in the head
- Swelling in the back of his head.
- Swelling all over the face area
- Broken bones in the face.
- Bloodied clothes from all the cuts and bruises.

None of the above happened. The accused had brushed himself off and was ready to get back to regular work the next day.

Bright and early the following day, when the world saw the accused; he did not look like a man who was having trouble with his faculties. His memory was sharper than any two-edged sword in his account of the events the night before and when it was time to walk the investigators through the crime scene; they had trouble keeping up with him! His steps were quick and accurate.

His memory of the deadly event with Trayvon, was delivered with great clarity. He drew a map of the crime scene even though it was dark and he was supposed to have been knocked unconscious that evening. He remembered exactly how he held Trayvon's hands out waiting for the police to come and arrest him, even though the poor boy wasn't even moving because he was already dead.

He remembered everything from last evening, didn't he? Well he remembered how Trayvon held down his mouth with one hand and kept punching his head and face with the other. And after that event Trayvon held him by the shoulders and bashed his head on the concrete over 20 times. He tried to scream but Trayvon held down his mouth and of course; he didn't want to bit Trayvon's hand to get it off his mouth so he grabbed his gun…the rest is history.

Ladies and gentlemen, many people were asking; is The accused really going to get away with murder, after contradicting himself so many times? Many believed that he lied to the police at the crime scene, and evidently; the accused did lie to the dispatcher when he gave the impression that he wasn't in pursuit of the person he called a suspect.

When a person lies, it means that he/she has some thing to hide. So what is it that The accused was and is hiding? Will he remain in a sound state of mind long enough to come forward to the public and said here is the truth about what really happened on that February night when Trayvon lost his life…

HE DROVE PASS TRAYVON…

In his report to the investigators; the accused said he drove pass Trayvon going the opposite way, then he noticed Trayvon had turned around and was following his vehicle. He parked his vehicle near the CLUB HOUSE, while he sat in it, Trayvon circled his vehicle and then walked off into the bushes.

After a little while, the accused claimed; he got out of his vehicle and was walking down to the end of the street to get the name of the street, that was the time at which, Trayvon emerged from the bushes and attacked him.

I don't know if anyone but the Jurors bought that story, especially the part about going to check out the name of the street that he was on. There are only 3 streets in that Complex according to reports, and the fact that the accused lived in that area for over 3 years made his stories less credible. He had to have known the name of that street. Again, there was a reason why he had to lie.

Ok then, let's say that The accused side of the story is gospel truth, nothing but... Trayvon is not here to give his version of the event but I am willing to keep an open mind, here. When he drove past Trayvon, did he roll down his window and sling some nasty ugly racial slurs at Trayvon? Well... ? If the answer is yes, he did (assuming), that would then explain why Trayvon made the sudden turn around to go and check out who could be so nasty and so vicious. 'This person does not know me,' Trayvon must have thought, 'where he got the nerves to call me those things. I will go down there and teach that person a lesson.'
Then again, Trayvon is on his way to watch a game on TV; why bother to follow up on some racist comments; black kids hear those racial or bigoted comments all the time and he was alone.

This is where I am puzzled; which black kid in his/her right mind walking home in the dark would see a slow moving vehicle drove pass and then turned around to walk two minutes down the lane to check who was in that vehicle, just because he was called some kind of racial name (assuming that was what happened)?

Some people have suggested that teenagers will be teenagers (they are impulsive beings, some more than others. Most teenagers do hold the belief that they are invincible). Trayvon might have been provoked and he walked deliberately into the path of danger not knowing that it would have caused him his life. What do you think? Was that the case? Did Trayvon think he was invincible? His past does not suggest that type of behavior according to my research into his brief life.

Remember now, Trayvon never had a gun or a knife in his position, so what would have prompted him to take such a deadly gamble with his own life. There is no suggestion that the kid was on any mind-altering drug that night and he wasn't acting irrationally.
Mr. Martin believes that his son was in his right mind when he left his house to get a Skittle and a drink.

The young man got what he went to the store for and was on his way back home to watch a game of basketball. The truth is, even if he was a bad kid; he did not deserved to die, not like that and not so young; my God!!! He deserved to live like everyone else. Life is a precious gift from the Creator and no one has the right to take it from you, no one! Life is short as it is. People; YOU don't need to pull a gun on each other to get your point across. No! The way I see it is that we should all help each other to live a fulfilling life. You for me and I for you.

FIGHT? ...WHAT FIGHT?

This is the spot where I am willing to part ways with those who are insisting that a fight took place, said one observer. There was no fight, people, None! That is what reasonable thinking people are thinking…they don't believe that a fight was possible because the accused person was bigger and looks far more intimidating than Trayvon and he also had a gun.

OK.. for the sake of argument, let's say there was a fight close to the CLUB HOUSE; near where the accused claimed it to be. There he said he was sucker punched. I am assuming here that he fell to the ground and was unconscious, when he came-to or regained consciousness; he found out that Trayvon was sitting on top of him, beating the crap out of him.

Clearly, Trayvon is deserving of a medal, even in death, for beating up a man who was in training, lifting weights… building his muscles to stay fit and strong to be able to defend himself (MMA style). He was also training intensely because he wanted to become a COP in the near future.

The accused had the training and the gun; for him to allow a 17 year old kid to beat up on him like that he should be a-shamed of himself. Is he a man or a mouse? For what purpose was all that training? Was it just a waste of time or was his sucker-punch story another one of his quick - off-the head-top- lies, many people believe so.

Some people are asking, how can you tell that the accused is lying? Listen it does not matter how many times person tells the truth? The truth simply does not change but once a person starts out with a lie, it snow-balls... it is no wonder the accused could not remember the first thing he said about how Trayvon rushed him from behind the bushes (what bushes)? Those shrubs were no more that two feet high, a squirrel could not hide behind them.

On the day of the verdict, I came across many people who were very angry that the accused got away with murder. Those were law abiding citizens who were not afraid to be unruly...they were prepared to disrupt the movements of a big city.

People everywhere were asking questions like: How can this man just stands there, telling lies, top and bottom to save his own skin from jail. Why couldn't the justice system see through his lies?

He did the crime, they said. Man-up to what you have done and go do the time, that's what I was hearing from those around me.

Did The accused person just suddenly discover that life is precious and is worth living. Did he not think that Trayvon would have liked to have lived out his days before he pulled out his gun like some harmless toy then pointed it to the young man's heart, moments later; he was dead?

At this point, only the accused knows what he has done... Only he knows what could have been avoided, on that cold February night. This is what I know, said one observer; he can hide from man but he cannot hide from God or himself.

At no point after the shooting did the accused ever looked truthful, many, many people from around the Globe were saying. Truth equal honesty, it does not change, it is not selfish and it does show remorse; the accused never displayed any of those qualities, from the night he killed Trayvon 'till the end of the trial. It was all about himself. He was the victim (so he claimed). He was the one that was assaulted, on that February night. He did not go looking for trouble, he said, trouble came looking for him.

Since the first day of investigation by the police until this present hour; the accused has not given a credible enough explanation as to why he felt the need to pursue Trayvon. The young man was clearly not a threat to him.

He never gave a credible explanation as to why he was at the bottom and Trayvon was on top of him covering his mouth with one hand and using the other to beat the crap out of him.

Many people have found it very difficult to understand why Trayvon's blood was not all over The accused face and clothing, since Trayvon was shot while still sitting on top of him with his knee up against his arm pit. Let me guess here; his hands suddenly became free and he was able to push Trayvon off before any blood could drip down on his clothing (right)?

HIS TRAINER

Oh well, I guess' desperate times call for desperate measures but for The accused trainer to just sit there before him and looked him in the eyes and called him soft… no muscles…after one year of training; that must have been very difficult to listen to. It was not easy for me to listen to, so can you imagine how the accused must have felt, sitting there looking like a big slab of fat… a 300 pound mommy? …that must have been very hard for that accused, teenage-killer to take in.

How did he feel when the trainer said, on a scale of 1-10, he was point five (0.5) in strength and agility. What really was going through his heart and his mind at that moment? I felt it for him when the trainer kept repeating the word "soft" over, and over again. I looked at his demeanor and it was saying to his Attorney, next question please, next question! Get on with it, Sir.

PROSECUTION …MISSED OPPORTUNITIES

What the prosecution forgot to show was that no person could have screamed so clearly from the gut if someone was sitting on top of him (belly or chest area). Just let your friend or you wife sit on your belly (if you feel too soft, please be careful); now try screaming like as if your life depends on it. On the other hand, don't try it; you might choke on you own spit. For anyone who is willing to go through with that experiment; I guarantee that you will be coughing involuntarily; you might not be able to catch your breath so, keep the 911 number handy.

Whenever pressure is applied to the abdominal area, the body is going to respond negatively; unless you are in training and you deliberately tighten up the abdomen to absorb the stress. The accused was out of practice; he was soft. He had no belly muscles. It was impossible for him to tighten up.

Bear with me a little here. Let us walk back to where I have said to you that most people I spoke with do not believe that a fight had taken place and I have also based it on the fact that the accused contradicted himself on more that one occasions.

This is what I don't understand; was the accused so soft that he couldn't push Trayvon off? His hands were never tied up at anytime, that was my understanding. He was not paralyzed because the next day he was up and about, swinging both arms like a healthy human being. His speech was not handicapped.

This is what the accused wants us to believe: he was lying there on his back helplessly, looking like a 6 year old. For some God-unknown reason; he did not have the strength to roll either side to try and get Trayvon off balance; he did not try to push Trayvon off with his hand(s). I am not sure if he had sudden paralysis or his hands were trapped but while Trayvon was beating the crap out of him and at the same time had his mouth covered up, he wants us to believe that he was yelling for help because he was in fear for his life. Why was he not able to fight back like a man? Some people want to know.

Wait a minute, does that sounds logical? one observer asked. Even if the accused had only one hand that was freed, (in his testimony he did not talk about his hands being not free at any point) that would have been enough to push Trayvon off is belly or chest area. There is no good enough excuses that the accused can come up with to tell the world why he could not have helped himself while he was underneath, the observer continued.

The natural instinct of every living creature, is to fight back when threatened or attacked; Check it out for yourselves, it is true. One will never allow himself to be attacked repeatedly, unless he is unconscious.
From The accused account of things, he was in his right mind. How do I know that, you may ask, because he counted every blow to the head and face. Are you kidding me! He knew when the first blow landed to his head and face and he also knew when the last blow landed to his head and face.

Twenty plus punches to the face without fighting back; that does not sound right to me. It sounds more like the facts have been blown up like a hot air balloon. What am I saying (facts)? What facts? There were no facts, according to popular opinions! And, since there were no facts, it means that most, if not everything that the accused claimed to have happened on that February night was untruths. So then if everything was untruths, it means that there was a root cause...

I know you might be saying to yourselves, OK then, he lost me. What the heck is this guy trying to explain? Well then, here it is; the crux of my argument:
Again, What in the name of the Holy FATHER was The accused doing with his two hands while he lay there on his back crying for help like a frightened 6 year old and how did he manage to scream on top of his lungs when Trayvon was covering his mouth with one hand?

I am trying to picture, in my head what a grown adult looks like, lying flat on his back, getting beat up by a 17 year old young man with a bag of Skittle and a canned drink in his pocket. It caused me to wonder if he was just lying there on his back looking like one who is nailed to a cross. I can see him now; hands outstretched… free me from this cross some body! Or maybe he was choking on his own spittle as he slurred his speech…

Look ma; I can't use my hands.

No, maybe he was swatting mosquitoes with both hands, since it was getting dark.

After the accused had changed his stories countless times during the early stages of the investigation; people were asking: Who is gonna believe his flip-flopping stories? Which court of law would take that killer seriously, most of us thought but we were all wrong. The law did not give a 'darn' how many times the accused changed his stories neither did it show any concerns about which part of Trayvon's body the bullet ripped through or his right to life and/or his rights to a fair trial.

It might sound strange to many but it is factual: in the United States Of America there are some States that have passed laws which protect killers or people with criminal intentions, not the innocent. Well, that is exactly what many who have experienced the hands of injustice have said, over and over again. Unless you are a person of color, poor and living in the worst areas you won't be able understand the magnitude of the injustices these people have to deal with day in and day out.

It is very hard to rap one's brain around the fact that a country which should have been well advanced in showing justice to all her citizens, regardless of color… is stepping backward into the caveman's era… every - man for - himself mentality.

Can you imagine a law which says to a vicious killer like the accused; you are free to go even though the killer had confessed to shooting the young man through the heart… you are a free man… you did nothing wrong, the voice of the law echoed. Where are the laws that will protect people like Trayvon? Who is looking out for the innocent?

In spite of the doom and gloom which have surrounded this case from the beginning; I do believe that Trayvon still has the Creator God on his side and in due time he, (GOD) will unveil the truth and justice will be served for Trayvon and his family. NO CRIME WILL GO UNPUNISHED …doesn't matter how long it takes.

WAS TRAYVON SHOT BEFORE…911 CALL?

For all we know, Trayvon could have been already dead before the 911 call took place. the authorities should have done a thorough DNA testing of the accused truck. What if the accused held Trayvon at gun-point… pushed him inside his truck and told him to shut up… and brought him to the place where he finally killed him, anything is possible, some are saying.

Think of it; you are the night's watch man in an area you claimed that homes were broken into by young black men. Now on this certain night; you saw a black youth in the dark, a person you called a suspect wearing hoodie, You followed him until you caught up with him. What are the odds that you would greet him and walk by so he can roam the neighborhood without fear? Most people I have conversed with don't think that was likely.

When police officers approach someone; they always have their guns at the ready, especially, where young black men are concerned. A wanna-be cop is no different. He has something to prove. Maybe he had some people in authority he wanted to impress.

The accused had two flash lights and a gun. He was the only one of the two who was able to see his target clearly. He was the only one who had the ability to take dead aim at the heart and pull the trigger.

Did The accused walk up to Trayvon (knowing that he had only few minutes before the police arrive) with his gun in hand hidden behind him and say punk (he did use that word only a short while ago), what are you doing in this neighborhood…?

He grabbed Trayvon by the collar and held on; Trayvon was trying to pull away but he couldn't: This one is not getting away, might have been what the accused was thinking.

I can see Trayvon's eyes and mouth popped wide open, he was very nervous, that would have been a natural reaction for anyone in similar situation. Did he get a chance to fight back? Was he throwing desperate and wild punches to free himself from the firm grip of the accused person's strong hand. Does that explain why he got those small scrapes on the side of his head? How about his bloodied nose, was that caused by Trayvon's one- two punch? …to some people, that's laughable.
Trayvon was not a fighter. That is my understanding.

Here is a theory someone ran by me… The accused caught up with Trayvon, after he was told not to pursue him; he held him by his jacket and pull him up close using words like; sucker, you are dead tonight! Or, you are not getting away with this! Then he raised his gun to eye level, Trayvon saw it; that's when he begun to scream like a man in trouble, straight from the depth of his belly, with every muscle in his being.
Then slowly the accused lowered the gun to Trayvon's heart and maybe the gun discharged accidentally then again, maybe not.

I wondered what the accused muttered after he fired that deadly shot. Did he used some racial slurs as the teenager laid there dying… blood gushing from his innocent little heart? I wondered if Trayvon had even one second to say, Mom; I love you or help, dad, help!

After Trayvon was shot; he fell forward to the ground with his hand clutching—holding onto the numbing area of his heart.
I wondered if he pleaded desperately for his life before that deadly shot. Did he say, please don't do this! Did the gun man smile, feeling all powerful with a gun in his hand?
Did the accused panic?

Did Trayvon get a chance to ask his killer why… why do you want to kill me? What evil have I done to you? 'NO!'… 'You've got the wrong person,' TRAYVON might have said.

Did I take the wrong path back to my house…? am I in the wrong place…? is this a dream…?' his young mind might have wondered.

One would think that the young man should have had safe passage back to his house. That path that he took was not off limit, that's my understanding.

In previous reports, the accused had claimed that he is a responsible gun owner; so what happened here? What happened in this guy's life to make him become such a irresponsible gun owner and human being? What could have caused him to shoot this young boy straight in the heart? Why did Trayvon have to lose his life in this crazy, crazy way, are some of the questions I am hearing.

"You aimed for his heart, you murderer! and your bullet didn't miss. Are you happy now? Did you accomplish your goal as a night's watch man." Those were the words of an angry protester.

Can you really blame anyone for being very, very angry over such senseless death of a young, innocent boy. Can you blame the city for wanting to explode when young black men are shot down like wild boars

Here is another one of the accused person's bizarre claims; he told authorities that while Trayvon was lying there on the ground, bleeding profusely; he held his hands down on the grass – outstretched! waiting for help to come but the police statement said that Trayvon's hands were curled up under him—in his chest area.

Maybe it's just me but I can't see any one holding a dead body and fail to realize that it was a dead, lifeless, motionless body that he was holding down. Really now; did he expect the dead boy to just get up and ran off?

If you were paying close attention, you would have noticed that the accused child killer, had an answer for every time he tripped up. And the troubling thing here is; he has the law as his umbrella. He is looking very comfortable underneath it… very sheltered. He is looking more and more like the victim in this case.

COMMON SENSE CASE

The prosecution had it right when they unfolded this case as a common sense case. I have no doubt that even a pre-teen is able to tell you positively who he/she believes the instigator was. After listening to the evidence of the case, it is not difficult to tell which one of the two was most likely to start a fight, if there was any fight at all.

At this point; I don't see where it matters much who was on top or who was screaming. In my opinion; too much time was spent trying to analyses whose voice it was… made no sense at all, to me.

Let me just say this; the person who was screaming, was not lying flat on his back; that is my assessment. Do you remember what the accused said about who was screaming? He said that he was the one screaming and he was the one lying flat on his back, helpless. Now, is Trayvon here to dispute that claim? No! but I can tell you from experience that no person who was lying flat on his back could have screamed with such power from the debt of his belly with someone weighing more than a hundred pounds sitting on top of it.

What I would have liked the prosecution to do was, to get one of their guys to sit on top of a member from the defense team and let him try to scream like what we had heard on the tape. I would have hoped he would be smart enough to wear an adult pamper… they would have learned quickly that when someone sits on your belly it is not a nice thing. It feels like everything is ready to pop out from below the waist and above the waist.

Let's take a step back and see where this case got started, in regards to the prosecution gathering evidence to do right by Trayvon.

1. It was 45 days after, that the Sanford Police Chief announced that there were no grounds to disprove the accused man's story of the event:
2. The firing or stepping down of the lead detectives:
3. Mass rallies across the country to bring a second degree murder charge against the accused.
4. A disqualification and/or replacement of a couple Judges, after all that, the prosecution finally got its hands on the case. Was the case doomed from the start? I don't think so. I do believe however, that the prosecution had a few missed steps along the way like, why wasn't the lead witness, I called Miss J. prepped from top to bottom… Meaning: she needed to know what to expect from the defense. She needed to know how to answer a question properly and to sit up straight. She was destined for failure.

I am willing to guest that there was a lot of finger twisting when the prosecution realized that they came to bat when the other side was already half way through the game. They came late in the game and had to start afresh with their own investigations; that was not an easy thing to do and apparently, that was not their fault.

If this case was a sprint race, I would say that the prosecution stumbled badly out of the box but did recover to race enormously well to gain equal footing with the front runner near the finish line. I think the result was that close… it was difficult to tell who had crossed the finish line first. You may not agree with me but I do believe that the result could have gone either way. Again, common sense would have to be utilized, for that to have happened.

…PICK UP THE PACE

I am here on the outside looking in, watching this trial and begging the prosecution to pick up the pace (like millions of like-minded people around the world) but what is it that they could have done better that could have turned the case around in Trayvon's favor?

It would have been quite rewarding, I think, to see the detectives on that tragic night run some kind of test on the teenage killer, such as a complete drug test and other test to measure his mental state of being because it was obvious that something went wrong that night.

There were some protesters who have suggested that the accused may be part of a cult, where he had to kill a person to belong…Did the investigators look into that possibility?

Shooting someone through the heart like that could very well means some kind of satanic rituals. If that was not the case, let me just ask the accused one question here: taking the life of this innocent young person, was it worth all the negative attention you brought on his family and yours? What did you gain from it?

From what I had observed, during the course of the trial, the accused killer did not look right and he did not talk right. What I mean is, whatever came forth from his lips sounded premeditated and without remorse but the justice systems had failed to notice; thus, leaving the door wide open for a potentially sick man to walk out into a world that he might not be able to handle mentally..

Here is what some are asking: was the accused man on mind-altering drugs? Or did some blood vessels in his head swollen up rendering that section of the brain that deals with logics completely useless? Was he indeed asking for help but the system, in its ignorance, completely ignored him? Is the accused a mental case ready to explode at any moment? Who will be his next victim? Is it your child or your neighbor's child, who will it be? Those and other things we might never know about the accused; unless he comes forward and declare any mental issues he might be faced with and or be up front with what really happened between himself and Trayvon.

I have said it before; the accused will never find peace within himself until he comes clean and take responsibility for what he did on that cold February night.

Trayvon is dead but the accused man is alive, enjoying his God–given gift (assuming). Trayvon's life was also a gift from the Creator but the accused, took it away, so what does that make him?

> Unless he comes forward and confesses, he will forever be acting like a mad man, doing crazy things to himself and to those around him. His way of life will be affected greatly - altered in the most negative way because he did something in the dark, on that cold February night which was not right. He had done a great evil under the night sky that will and should haunt him 'till he takes his last breath.

PROSECUTION HAD GUTS

Let me reveal what some observers would have liked to see the moment the case was handed over to the prosecution… They should have taken their own investigative team to the crime scene, and recreate the whole thing just as the accused described it:

1. go inside the witnesses' home and recreate the scene from their vantage point (according to the evidence) and see for themselves if it was possible the way the accused described it.

2. they needed to check out the witnesses version of the event. Could they really see movements in the dark from where they were standing? Did they hear more or less than they were letting on. Could they have said more to help Trayvon?

3. set up some kind of audio in the home(s) of the person(s) who was on the phone with the 911 operator; test the audio from where they claimed to be standing. Could they really hear clearly from that distance?

4. Some people who were routing for justice did questioned if the prosecution had dug deep enough for information? Maybe they were too much on the surface sweeping with brooms when, at a time like that they should have been digging with forks (perhaps backhoe) and never stop until they reach pay-dirt?

5. get the mannequin out the first week. Show the Jury why you think it was impossible for Trayvon to be on top of the accused, beating the crap out of him and at the same time, holding down his mouth and nose.

6. show just how impossible it would have been for the accused to reach his gun with Trayvon on top of him and his knees pressing against his arm pit. Honestly; it sounded so silly that really, some people don't want to even think about it… don't want to hear it.

7. the accused man's recollection of the event really doesn't make much sense, some are saying but does he really cares what others think about him? Perhaps all that he cares about, at this point, is that the system buys into his stories, others have suggested. Once that happened; his path to freedom will be cleared.

TRAYVON USED ONLY ONE HAND…

Really now… how could a grown man just lie there, like dead, getting the beating of his life and according to his testimony; the kid only used one hand to beat him up from his head to his toes. No, sorry; from head to face. (because the kid used his other hand to hold down his nose and mouth), that is incredible. Did he expect anyone to believe that testimony? Apparently yes!

8. They would have liked the prosecution to show that it was possible that the accused could have held Trayvon at gun-point and told him to shut up!

and with the gun pointed at him; Trayvon was brought to the spot where he was shot dead. After he shot Trayvon, then the accused rubbed his jacket in the grass? Did he bash his own nose and head in with his own gun? Those were valid questions that some people were asking.

MINOR ABRASIONS ON HIS HEAD… WHAT'S UP WITH THAT?

9. Those two small cuts on his head, certainly didn't appear to be consistent with traumatic blows to one's head, some people suggested.
10. Well, listen; the accused went to great length to describe how Trayvon bashed his head against the pavement twenty times or more. Those two scrapes, I saw on his head really didn't represent his description of the altercation.

11. The eighteen year old witness, Miss J (I wish to call her that for now) was not deserving of the treatment she got on the witness stand. I would have liked the prosecution to have prepped her to the max. She would have made an excellent witness from what I saw of her in later interviews.

12. I would have liked to see the prosecution object a lot more to the vigorous questioning by the defense. The truth is; Miss J. did not lie to cover up anything about the case. She had just lost her friend. Any person, young or old would have been shocked to learn of the sudden death of a friend whom you were on the phone with, moments before he met his tragic end.

So she lied about her age, why? because she did not want to be in a courtroom with millions of people scrutinizing her every move and her slowness of speech. Miss J. knows better than anyone that she does not have a good command of the English language. I believe, in spite of her short-comings, she would have made an excellent star witness for her friend, Trayvon, if the prosecution had prepared her properly.

Finally, Since Trayvon was on top (as was claimed…) I would have liked to hear the defense explanation as to why, all that blood from the wound was not spilled out onto the accused. His jacket was as clean as a whistle. His clothing, neck and face area did not have not a single trace of Trayvon's blood. What's up with that? There is no way he could have pushed Trayvon off in time without getting blood being spilled all over him, said one observer.

Given what the prosecution had to work with, in such short space of time, however; they deserved to be applauded for their efforts, they really deserved high marks for guts.

The prosecution took the case knowing very well that the odds were stacked up high against them. They came at the last minute and argued like the professionals they are. In my humble opinion, they seemed to have poured out their hearts and soul into this case to bring justice to a dead young man and his family. I raise my glass to them.

FURTHER MORE...

Look at what the prosecution had to put up with:
1. A defense team that had a head start...
2. The defense got to pick their own Jury
3. The defense got to eliminate a lot of testimonies that were in favor of Trayvon.
4. It appeared as though the defense had the influence over which Judge sat on the bench! according to reports.

They seemed to be the only team who could have made a funny knock- knock joke about the case and got away with it, in that courtroom. It appeared as if they were telling us (the public) oh, this case is a no-brainer.

THE VERDICT

I know for sure that the prosecution was getting beaten up badly (in the eyes of the Jury) but I was still hoping that common sense would have prevailed because this was not a case where one had to dig too deep to find the truth.

The accused had confessed to the killing. That was a jury Stack with women (one good thing for the prosecution we had hoped). Those women have children, they might show compassion to the dead boy's mother; that was the general thinking but we were all wrong. The case was more complex than how it was first perceived.

When people around me (friends and family) were saying, no way… it's all over, I was staying positive. I was staying positive! It was such a revealing murdering case, starting from who was the instigator that led up to the murder to, where is all the DNA that should have been on Trayvon's hands since he had beaten down so much on this big guy, with soft muscles. What was really going on with all the missing pieces and inconsistencies? It is anyone's guess.

When the prosecutor got on top of the mannequin, we all said "yes!" They've heard us, finally. we was calling for that demonstration from day one!

Where have you guys been with that…? Show them the knee up against the armpit, there is no way he could have shot Trayvon from that position…. Yes! Show them that it was impossible for the accused to reach his gun in the manner in which he described that Trayvon was sitting on top of him. Yes! Show them that it was impossible for Trayvon to hold that big guy by the shoulders and smash his head more that twenty times on the concrete. Yes! Show them. Yes! Show them! The demonstration was excellent but there was one big problem facing the prosecution; the Jurors were fast asleep, the defence knew it but there weren't about to wake them up.

I was at a friend's house and you should have seen us... All of us had suddenly became educated debaters and lawyers. We were all sure now that the prosecution had finally driven the truth (in its simplest form) home at last, to a Jury that might not have been paying much attention to their common sense presentation of the case.

So when the verdict was read next evening, we were more than a little shocked... wings were clipped.. jaws dropped. Somewhere, in the back of my mind, I had few questions to ask... one was; have a civilized society lost the meaning of the word JUSTICE? (2) how much MORE can BLACK AMERICANS endure? Honestly, I think the Martin family was expecting better from this all-white Jury of 6-1.

I think my biggest shock came from the word; unanimous. It was like, what da...? Talk about consciences scorched with a hot iron. Talk about cold and heartless. Where was the humanity? Those 6 never heard of the word common sense? The question is, do they even know the meaning...? Well... maybe one did, according to her live Television explanations, not long after the verdict, that her hands were tied by the Judicial system - she had no other choice but to go along with the rest to deliver a not guilty verdict for a murderer.

No disrespect to the Jury system, some people have said. but they think history is going to revisit this decision and agree that it was very harsh especially for the Martin family and others who have experienced similar fate.

Most of the people I spoke to thought at least we would have seen a hung Jury or something like: 2 against, 4 in favour. Any other result would have been more palatable and the accused might have still walked, but at least it would have left people saying they were really in there fighting for the kid.

The Jury, I thought would have most assuredly gave some thoughts to the victim, considering the circumstances that surrounded his death. Look at it! He was coming from the store, for God's sake. Probably hop-scotching home. Well…! what would you be doing as a 17 year kid…? I am sure he was happy to be spending time with his father and he was talking to his girl friend, on his way back from the store. I am pretty sure that there was some sense of excitement being back in that area.

In retrospect of the event; the young man did not have a death wish, and as far as I know; he did not threaten to kill anyone. The last thing of importance, I believe, that was on his mind, was to get back home and watch a game of basket ball.

He was deserving of better. For Law makers, I say this; he spoke from the grave and you did not listen. Those who could have done something positive about this tragedy; you have all closed your ears from hearing the truth and your bowels of compassion… there was none.

After the trial, it became evidently clear that, one of the Jurors was struggling with her conscience about setting a murderer free. Once again, a law that was designed to suppress the rights of Minorities (particularly Blacks) bound her by the wrists so that she was not able to check off guilty (guilty as death itself) which could have meant the beginning of the end to this killer's freedom. People around me were saying; "he took an innocent life and he must pay the price… you cant do the time; don't do the crime".

Juror B29, said she voted to convict the accused of second degree murder on the first day of deliberation but on the second day she realized that she was up against the law which stated that they (the Jurors) had to see proof that the accused intentionally killed Trayvon. Now a week or two later she has said that she is having a difficult time sleeping at nights. It is also very difficult for her to eat because she felt she was forcibly involved in Trayvon's death. She might have been the only one with a live conscience in that Jury room and to that I say it is a darn shame.

THE ACCUSED WAS NERVOUS

When the Verdict was read, I could see a nervous man (the accused) tightened up some, trying desperately to hold off that explosive smile that is associated with self-accomplishments, a win or a victory in one's endeavours. He did expose his pearly whites for a bit but he did not expose his heart; what is in there? People are wondering. What is in your heart? Maybe the question should be; do you have a heart? Is there one inside that building of yours?

What a pity. Trayvon will never get the chance in this lifetime to tell his side of the story. Trayvon will never graduate or work in the educational field of his choosing. He will never get a chance to date and or get married. He will never have children and watch them grow. He will never experience what it is like to share in the joys and the sorrows of life, its ups and downs, its peeks and valleys.

If only all human beings were sain; life would be perfect, I think. Then again; maybe we are not all human beings. Some individuals look, walk and talk like every other humans but the things that they do would suggest otherwise. Individuals like Hitler, Charles Manson, Dahmer. Jack the Ripper, Son of Sam, those are some of the individuals who took great pleasure in raping and killing women and children. Those are some of the dedicated mass murderers who, a person has to truly wonder which race they are from.

Some murderers are known for eating human hearts and other human's body parts just for the pleasure of it, would you call those humans. A person who looked another person and shot him through the heart, for no apparent reason at all, would you call him a human being?

…NOT SO HAPPY MOMENTS

People around the Globe, lovers of justice, had their wings clipped when the Verdict was read… Unanimous decision… not guilty! There was a sigh of relief, however; when we had learned that the Martin family was not at the court house for the reading of the verdict, it was a very wise decision on their part not to be there. Wisdom had spoken and they listened.

Many people I know still cannot understand why it took the Jurors 16 hours of deliberation to make their decision, after having had 14 days of testimonies. They had listened to what made sense and to what made no sense at all. Don't tell me that they didn't already make up their minds half way through the trial. Didn't one of the Jurors say that they were more assured of their decision once the lead Detective had testified? Oh yes. She went on to say, The detective knew what he was talking about. He deals with those types of cases on a daily basis (that was their perception) he believed in the accused and so do we, she continued. That was just too frightening to hear.

Well, what can I say. The Jurors have spoken and if anything other than the truth hand influenced their decision, they will have to live with that for the rest of their lives.

UNIQUE CASE

Personally; I have not heard of a similar case like this one... A boy left his house to buy skittles and a drink, was trailed by a neighbourhood watch man who then shot him in the heart; he fell dead. So where does this detective get off saying that he deals with that sort of crime all the time; that is what many are asking. And to rub salt into the wound; a great portion of the population is willing to forgive the accused for his heinous crime, it is a tragedy.

Where the heck are you heading America? More appropriately, where is this entire world heading? One thing I know, if the head of the stream is muddy; one cannot expect that the bottom of it will be clean.

Is there any hope for the human race? Is the future of this entire generation heading to hell in a hand basket?

A SHOUT OUT TO YOUNG BLACKS...

I am writing this book for all black men, especially young black men, to take note: work hard for what you want and teach your children to do the same. Stop robbing and killing! Stop breaking and entering! Stop taking what is not yours! Stop it!

Let society judge you by your good actions. Your good deeds will speak for you. Live within your means. You don't have to rob and kill anyone for things that do not belong to you.

This is how most white people look at people of colour: blacks are involved in most of the crimes; they are all the same. No; we are not all the same. It would be stupid for black people to say all white people are racist; that would not be true!

The accused took it up on himself to profile Trayvon when he said, they always get away with it. Right away, he was assuming Trayvon was like the criminals who are breaking into people's homes or those who are out there robbing local stores.

Listen, it is a good thing to be a neighbourhood watch man. Yes it is a good thing to watch out for the bad guys because there are some who love to take things they did not put down… like to break into homes they don't own… like to reap what they don't not sow. However, being a watch man for your neighbourhood, does not give you the right to profile and take someone's life for no apparent reason. If you see someone acting suspiciously, your duty is to call the police.

The accused did the right thing by calling 911 but, wait a minute; who was he trying to fool? asked one protester. He might have made that call to cover his tracks, in committing the perfect crime, he suggested. Well not so perfect, I do think, there were few mistakes here and there…

Listen; it is all well and good to watch out for your neighbourhood but don't go playing the hero by hurting or killing someone to make yourself look good.

Life is this remarkable, one-time gift from God, no one has the right to take it from you and I believe human beings should help each other to live their lives to its fullest, honestly; I don't think it is hard to do.

Who does not want to grow up to exercise their choices in life: have kids, live a long healthy life, make plans, get rich, retire at 35, throw plenty of parties. No one has the right to take those things away from an individual, no one! What is the conclusion of the whole matter? Let us be our brother's keepers. Let us make peace, not war.

This might be the greatest chance we get as world leaders and citizens to get rid of the old laws and old ideas and start afresh with news laws and new ideas.

For two thousand years the old laws and ideals never were successful in moving nations in the right direction, that is; cultivating love, peace and harmony and success for their citizens and future generations. Instead they have cultivated fear and anarchy, poverty and misery, guns and wars. The time is right for change. I pray to God that law

makers will grab hold of this opportunity for posterity's sake.

No longer should a person's skin colour determines his or her success in life. It is time all the nations around the Globe, not just the USA, get away from the present racist culture. Only then will real and lasting prosperity be realized.

DOES THE JURY SYSTEM WORK?

Well, The greater percentage of the population will tell you that the system doesn't work for them; doesn't work for their friends; it doesn't work for their families…it's a failure, they believe.

Look… Take a case such as this one: Trayvon Benjamin Martin's. Six Jurors, minus one minority. So the assumption was (by the prosecution) that they would have used common sense in their decision making and boy, oh, boy; was the prosecution ever wrong. Well; one of the Jurors did come on TV and said she wanted to vote the other way but she was forced to join up with the other five white Jurors. The way the Law is written does not make it very easy for Jurors to rule in favour of the victims, that's my understanding.

In this era of enlightenment and rationality; no reasonable person would have imagined that a country as rich and educated, such as these United States of America, would be so bogged down over issues concerning laws which don't solve problems but instead, create problems for those who are nothing less that upright citizens.

WHAT A JUBILATION...

The defence was beside themselves, during the trial, then again, why not? They knew the kind of case they were working on. The case was handed to them on a gold platter. They got to pick the JURORS and, like bad apples amongst good; they got to toss out the bad ones--- the rejects (they were very good at spotting the sympathetic ones).

People on the outside could see clearly how much fun the defence was have. Given the easy time they had with the witnesses and most of all it would seem like they were able to sway all the prosecution witnesses to their side.

Did anyone check to see if there was any powder-like stuff sprinkled near the witness' box. VOODOO powder maybe. No, just joking.. no such thing as VOODOO powder/power. Well... that was just an observation. Can't take a little humour? OK then what else could have been the cause of it...?

Remember the medical examiner, how he carried on...? 'I don't remember anything; zero. I, depend only on my notes.. that's why I brought my notes...? That was some strange behaviours!!!! Check for powder residue, I am telling you. Ha, ha, ha. Check!

Here comes the defence.. 'sir can I have those notes...? I am serious sir, can I have your notes...' dear God, I said; another one bites the dust for the prosecution.

Remember Sanford Police Department's chief investigator? he told the jury he believed the accused man's account was truthful. He had doubted his stories before and wanted to bring charges against him but something happened in the courtroom that caused him to switch sides from the prosecution to the defence, what happened? Look! Is that an OBeyah/ (science) man sitting next to the Martins lawyers, someone joked.

    Even after the defence Attorney made a fool of himself, smashing the head of the mannequin repeatedly on to the floor, the Jury still was not convinced that it was not possible for Trayvon to smash the accused head (for some 20 times) against the concrete. Good God! Where would Trayvon get the strength to hold a big guy like that by the shoulders and smash his head like a rag doll.

    Now look at the Attorney for the prosecution, he got on top of his mannequin and put his knees up against its arm, just like the accused described how Trayvon was on top of him. He asked the witness, could the accused have reached his gun with Trayvon on top of him like so…..? He grudgingly said, no but the Jurors fell asleep during that demonstration.

What a contrast; he (prosecution) showed the fact, undisputed.. comparing to the impossible task the defence had demonstrated earlier and it was like everyone else in the room had just had a shot of 100 proof White Rum.

How on God's green earth can anyone hold an opponent by the collar and smash his head repeatedly into the ground… sidewalk, or wherever, and what did the witness say to that abuse of the mannequin.. during the defence's demonstrations? yes, it was possible; Trayvon could have done that…

WHO WAS ON TOP?

DOES IT MATTERS?

Earlier I told you that I do not believe for one second that there was a fight between those two but let's say there was… trust me on this one; it does not matter who was on top or bottom because, not even Andrea The Giant (one of the great wrestlers over 500 lbs) could have managed to smashed a 200 pound young man's head on-to the concrete 19+ times, neither was it possible to scream from the gut lying flat on one's back with a hundred and fifty pounds sitting on top of it.

Everyone is angry at this verdict. Well...almost everyone. the accused is not angry, he is happy, gleeful in fact because he sensed that the law is going to cover his murderous heart but soon he will know for sure, that it cannot cover his guilt neither can it cover his pains, those he will have to live with until the day he takes his last breath looking upon the ceiling of his own heart, remembering, in those dying moments, how he wasted a young life for no apparent reason.

COMMON SENSE

Common sense! Common sense. It was just a common sense case and if the Jury was thinking of Trayvon, the majority of viewers was expecting them to come with a Verdict that might read like this: we the Jury could not come to a unanimous decision... 2 against and 4 in favour; 1 against and 5 in favour. Something like that would tell the public that they had Trayvon in mind when they came to their decision of not guilty. Having done that, I think Trayvon would be saying, from his heavenly places: there is hope yet...there is hope for the human race... but can that be said in this case and so many other cases where justice was not evenly cut for some people, black or white? Well, mostly blacks, I am sure.

The defence was beside themselves with joy when the Verdict was read. Well the correct quote here is, 'ECSTATIC.' Not only were they ecstatic but one member of the team said, the accused was not guilty of anything except protecting himself. Well! Talk about rubbing salt into the wound. The very person who created the problem and who is the causation of another person's death is now hailed as protecting himself? And don't anyone feel sorry for the accused because he was told not to follow or pursue the person he called suspicious.

Wait for the police, the voice pleaded… The police will deal with the matter but the accused decided to take matters into his own hands.

How do you think Trayvon felt when he said to his girl friend; 'I have been followed by a 'creepy-ass cracker.' Then, just before his cell phone went dead, he asked, "what are you following me for?" and then yelled, "get off, get off." Get off!!! What did Trayvon mean when he said that? Well, some people think at that instance, the accused could have been up in Trayvon's face or that could have been the very moment when he forced Trayvon to the ground and sat on top of him.

Well, just imagine that you have just heard your friend on the phone said, 'somebody is following me' and then seconds later you heard him saying; 'get off, get off.' Personally; I would have thought, my friend is in trouble, serious trouble. There was no longer any communication between Trayvon and his friend. That was the very moment when Trayvon met up with the devil.

Oh, yes! The devil is real. This time he poked his head out from his hell hole and snuffed out another innocent life because he knew Trayvon was never gonna be part of his organization and he didn't like that. He knew that Trayvon would be a light to illuminate the way for his generations to come and he didn't like that.

Let me say this, not ever person who walks our streets are real human beings, there are some who are demons, agents of the devil…monsters. Their real purpose on earth is to disrupt and be disruptive. They are always planning and scheming how to destroy the innocents… the unsuspecting good Samaritans – the Mother TERESA(S) or the MARTIN LUTHER KING(S) of the world but thank goodness; light will always illuminate darkness, good will always overcome evil.

For those of you who had to face the demons of the world; we feel your pains; we mourn with you; we cry our eyes out for you from our small corners.

Many people believe that the accused had hastened his pace with fire in his eyes; caught up with Trayvon, grabbed him by the hoodie and spun him around and when they finally came face to face; he raised his gun up to eye level to keep Trayvon quiet; but he was too scared to be kept quiet; that's when, some believe, that Trayvon screamed from his belly, whoohoie!!!!!! At no time would you ever hear a white person screamed like that; that was the scream of a black person… woo as in woooo (cow) ho-- i,(short i). deep from his belly, that was the scream of death.

Again, common sense was all it would have taken to bring truth to the senseless death of a wonderful (as his parents would describe him) young man, and a wonderful son.

No one was going to believe Rodney King if the camera wasn't there. Now who is gonna believe Trayvon Martin with out a camera being THERE, not the authorities and certainly not the Jurors (6).

SYSTEMS NEED TO BE CHANGED

If America is to prosper among the nations, the legal systems have to be changed. No one is saying that the United States of America has not made great strides in improving race relations with blacks and other minorities since the sixties but there still seems to be some underlying issues of honesty and trust between people of colour and Law Makers; those issues are like cancer cells that are eating away at the healthy areas of the country, so in essence; the country is not able to move forward in providing everyone with the same opportunities, regardless of colour.

Not since the murder of 14-year-old Emmett Till, who was killed in 1955 after supposedly whistling at a white woman "and whose murderers were acquitted:" have a people been so outraged at the miscarriages of justice across the land.

I have asked the question, does the Jury system work? Many people of colour don't really think so. In my opinion, the only time the system will work is when you have honest responsible people sit - in as Jurors. They should be people who can think for themselves in stressful situations…, not easily swayed by others.

JURORS SAT ALONE WITH FAMILY…

What I believe the legal system should not allow is to let Jurors sit one and one with their families for hours and that is exactly what happened in Trayvon Martin's case.

It was reported by the Seminole County Sheriff's Office that the Judge in charge allowed Jurors to spend up to 2 hours with family members. Who knows if those Jurors heard more than they should have about the case. There is no doubt that even a little whisper about what was going on with the case could have influenced their decision making.

THE AFTERMATH

When the leaders of these United States look at their own citizens and ask, why are we not prospering? Why are there so many bankruptcies across the land? Why is the crime rate so high? They should stop pointing fingers at other nationalities whom they have blamed for taking away American jobs and put undue hardship on the economy and other areas of the system. I believe that the politicians and law makers need to look themselves and ask; what are we doing wrong? Surely, they must have read it somewhere, that a nation divided against itself cannot stand.

Again, it's only a common sense solution to what seems like it is such a huge mountain of problems: give equal opportunity to all citizens of the land and the country will prosper. Don't covet the growth of your citizens… that will eventually create poverty, which eventually leads to strife and the disruption of generous production across the board.

Stop holding on to things that do not benefit the nation. Stop putting stumbling blocks in the way of your people. Stop turning your heads away from the problems. America! You have got to wake up!

The sad thing here is that if America catches a cold, the whole world coughs but how long can the world wait for America to lead by example.

GOD IS IN THIS…

Remember at the beginning I said to you that God is in this? I think from here on in, if the Martin' family was ever feeling let down by their faith, they should take comfort in knowing that they have found favour with the Creator to bring about change in America.

The death of Trayvon Martin has brought out an even greater awareness among the people, black and white that no longer will the death of a young black person which may have been caused by law enforcement officer(s) go unnoticed. There is a great awakening to rise up and be heard.

No country or people can expect to reap peas if they sow corn. No nation can prosper when its leaders are dishonest to their own citizens (in this case, some citizens).

How will the nation be healed when a member of the defence team is always showing up on TV and making comments like; only people who are closed minded cannot accept the accused version of the event of February 26, 2012 or, the accused has a right to his firearm now more than ever because there are some out there who desire his hurt and he did nothing wrong. All he did was defended himself.

Trayvon is not around to give his side of the story; so somebody has to stand up for him. Somebody have to pick sense out of non-sense. The real non-sense in this case is for them to still be defending a man who was in no position to pursue Trayvon with a loaded firearm. It was an illegal thing to do. Can they not see that it was wrong! Are they so blind? I wonder why? He was not the police. He was not even a hired security guard.

A BIG SORE…

There is a big sore, deep in the American psyche which has been festering for many years and it had to break open; it had to be exposed like a Volcano that has blown its lid, spewing lava violently down stream and far up into the skies.

None of us know for sure what really happened in the darkness of that night when Trayvon lost his life. None of us know for sure the motive(s) behind it but one thing we know for sure is that the rottenness of the system has been exposed once again in a very big way and the stink of it has been wind-swept to the four corners of the earth.

Look at it this way… God still loves the United States of America, I believe. He still has a people there; that could very well be the reason why he is giving Politicians and Law Makers another chance to redeem themselves…to right the wrongs of the past. Only then will prosperity be realized… the country will then rise to greatness, honour and respect or it will fall off the cliff like the great Babylon.

It is very unfortunate that this tragic situation has taken on some political and racial overtones. Those people who are trying to change the main conversational point need to stop it and focus on the real issues at hand… not all people are treated equally under the law… that is not up for debate.

There are laws that were made with one goal in mind: to suppress the growth of a great many people, who through no fault of their own happen to have a different skin colour other than white. It is sad indeed, not just for this generation but for future generations.

I believe that if the broken Laws can't be fixed, then Law makers and politicians need to tie a millstone around them and toss them into the middle of the seas and Enact new laws to serve all the people justly.

When all the people can find themselves with equal opportunity to grow and prosper in the field of their choice; I have no doubt that criminal activities will decrease significantly over the years and these United States of America will be the greatest nation on earth because deep down, they (U.S. Citizens) are a generous people always ready to lend a helping hand to people around the world.

SUMMARY

Can we all just get along?
honestly!

When I hear those who claimed to be professional analyst saying publicly that people should have an open mind towards the accused which would make it much clearer to see why he did what he did on that February 26 night; it made me feel like jumping out of my skin.

I don't know, quite honestly, if those analyst and debaters know more than they are letting on. Do they know the truth about that night and have it in their mouths swirling around like chewing gum, chewing and spitting out, chewing and spitting out? Whatever the result, they should stop defending that killer. it is very disturbing. When you think of it, why have an open mind towards the accused and not the same for Trayvon?

Trayvon is dead but he has a right to a fair trial. he has a right to be heard. Why does the defence still insist on suppressing the rights of this young man?

When you as analyst and debaters go on national television and tell the world to have an open mind towards the accused because all he was doing out there that night was defending himself, it means that you know exactly what happened but I am not ready to believe that anyone, aside from the accused knows exactly what took place out there, on that chilly February night. So lets call your talkativeness, a side show for the Media; you have to keep them honest, I get it!

Some how, I am getting the distinct feeling that the defence don't want anything to do with Trayvon's side of the story and we all know that there are two sides to every story. Trayvon is not here to tell his side but the evidences around him are speaking loud and clear but people in authority are not willing to listen!

The accused man was not the police; he was not a hired security guard; who gave him the right to pursue the young man with a loaded gun? Why have the educated ones closed their minds to the truth? There are people out there whose only wish is, that every time those lawyers see the truth, in this Trayvon Martin's case and closed off their minds towards it, that they should have a sudden rush of diarrhoea, at the place where they are standing when they deny Trayvon of his rights to a fair trial. Well, I don't know... would that be enough?

ABOUT THAT NIGHT

About that night; it is clear, evidently clear that the accused did not identify himself as the neighbourhood watch man. If his thoughts were pure, that would have been the first thing he would have done.

Those f—ing punks…

they always get away with it..

and why were the previous 911 calls he made always about blacks…?

The injustices that black people experience every day are the reasons why they have to yell hard and long, said one observer. There are two sides to a story but only one side is listened to and it is not the black side of it, he continued.

It is obvious that black people are the ones who know what it feels like to being watched constantly, when they are out shopping: in the malls, corner stores, etc., especially young blacks.

When black people scream out in pain because they have been treated with injustice; others ought to stop making faces; stop talking, stop pointing fingers and stop calling black people names and listen to their complaint… feel their pains and their hurts.

I have for a long time now realize that there are some people out there who look like humans but they are not humans; so I don't expect those kinds to know how to share pains and emotions. I expect them to continue to say black people are monkeys and chimps. I expect them to continue to make funny faces.

Black people are very familiar with being treated unfairly; legal lynching, church bombings, vigilante killings, in much of that; many of the killers walked free. Remember about those four black girls who were attending Sunday school in Birmingham, more fifty years ago? …the pain is deep.

Don't get me wrong here. You will find thieves out there who are unconscionable and you will find them in every culture but blacks have been singled out, more like vultures. The black man or woman can be spotted from miles away, what is the cause for all that: the system. Change the system… change the culture…, people will feel respected and in-turn will show respect.

WHO WAS ON TOP?

I made it quite clear that it did not matter who was on top or who was screaming, because there was no fight as the accused has claimed. None, some people believe.

The screaming did not come from someone lying on his back. the screaming we heard came from someone who saw a gun and was feeling threatened, who wanted to escape but could not... that might have very well explain why the hoodie touched the point of the gun.

If there was no fight that means that there was no bashing of the head to the concrete; there was no sitting on the belly; then there were no knees up against the accused armpits, all lies.... people around me are saying...lies, lies, lies, from top to bottom; based on the evidence of the killer, many people agreed. The accused needs to own up to his evil deeds. He was armed with a loaded gun and 2 flashlights. The teenager only had in his pocket or in his hands a bag of Skittles and a canned drink, walking home to watch a game of Basketball. The night watchman (the accused) pursued the teenager and shot him dead. At this point, only he knows why.

Radio Personalities/TV Hosts

Some of you need to zip your lips and do it fast because you are stirring up filth. When you get on the air waves to say that race has nothing to do with this, Trayvon Martin saga, you need to examine your dialogues. I am very sure that if Trayvon was some other colour; he would not have been profiled, ok. Who was the accused talking about when he said, they always get away with it? Race might not be the main issue in this case but it was certainly one of the issues.

PRESIDENT OBAMA

The President, your President, is not just a man; he holds the highest office in the Country and he represents the whole nation. If you don't respect the man, at least respect the office. I feel ashamed for some of you; trying to elevate yourselves above the office.. trying to make yourselves look good. Who are you? A country is not made up of one person and you are not bigger than the country!

Why don't some of you watch what you are saying? If you think that you can run the country better than President Obama; why don't you run for the office! see if you are man/woman enough to fill the President's shoes.

Considering that many of you have been blocking his path since day one and to see what he has accomplished in less than six years, as the first black president; I doubt that any one of you can fill his shoes, for the next 1000 years. Well, 1000 years might be a little extreme but just saying…, work with your President; strength is in numbers.

When you sat there (as radio hosts) and tell me and the world that the President should find something better to talk about instead of wasting time on this Trayvon Martin saga because there have been worse shootings in your cities and black men are always shooting up black men and their deaths never got this kind of spotlight.. it showed me that you have missed the point totally and you should not be on television or radio expressing your reckless thoughts. You should be home tending to your BBQs… enjoying your burgers and whatever beverages you might have to go along with them. The back yard is where you belong, not on Radio or Television, trying to stir up trouble.

When you as a black radio hosts sat there telling the world that the president is no better than the accused; the only difference (in your words) is that he's got a bigger audience; it left me speechless. I am not sure what to think about people like you; is it that you want to be controversial or you have just pissed all over yourselves.

There is no magic bullet in solving the Country's problems. The President does not work alone. He does not have the power to stand on top of the highest mountain and wave a wand over the country and magically bring healing to her, from her years of diseases, which some of the leaders in her past have brought upon her.

What some of you blinded demagogues need to know is that her healing has begun. Stop talking negatively and let the healing continue. Stop spitting up on your chest in ignorance. Not one of you out there is worthy to fill President's shoes.

Trayvon Martin's death is a blessing in disguise it would appear because it has brought out a lot of positive conversations which the nation can start to build on. No one is saying his death is the only thing that is deserving of the spotlight, no! nobody is saying that at all, but it was a unique event in the sense that the gravitational pull was extremely far to one side.

The whole world felt the injustice dealt to the Martin's family; after the system had said to them; 'we have found no grounds on which to lay charges against the accused. Sorry for your loss but this murderer is free to go.' Would you have taken that sort of response lying down, if Trayvon was your son or relative?

I think that there are some great and wonderful things that are about to happen in everyone's lives because of Trayvon's death. No! it is not the resurrection of the black and white issues. No, it's not the regular… "can we all get along" question or the racial injustice speeches. seriously, those issues… it is like beating a dead horse; you can't beat it any more…it wont move! But it is this enormous surge in awareness that if this present world is going to move forward in one piece; then we must all be our brothers keepers. We must all look out for each other.

THE ACCUSED WILL BE HAUNTED…

There are some people who believe that the accused will be haunted for the rest of his life because he refused to come forward and owned up to what really happened that night when he shot young TRAYVON dead.

Most people refused to speak through the corner of their mouths when it comes to the accused telling his side of the story. They don't believe that the accused spoke one word of truth in defending himself.

He really Does seem like one who is trying very hard to hide something of importance. Some people think that he is trying his best to keep a tightly shut lid on his volcanic situations but there is so much steam bursting through…, at any time now there could be some big explosions.

From what I saw in court each day; he appeared to me as one who is ready to free his soul of a heavy burden, that might not mean that he is thinking of Trayvon's death. Maybe he had other personal issues on his mind but he really didn't look healthy in body or in spirit.

TROUBLE WITH THE LAW

Soon after the accused was found not guilty of Trayvon's death he started to experience regular run-ins with the law: pulled over 3 times for traffic violations, ticketed for doing 60 in a 45mph zone, arrested for domestic violence where guns were allegedly involved (more than once), his mother – in law filed a police report that he stole her furniture and TV. His wife said he should have been charged with Trayvon's murder; she now believes he is guilty, and, to add to his woes; his wife also filed for divorce, according to news reports.

Since those events; most people are now saying that the accused might very Well be haunted by the death of Trayvon Martin. Don't forget that one's conscience can be like hell… a ball of fire deep in the psyche.

If the accused wants to save his own sanity; he has to look deep within himself and ask; did I leave out crucial information about what took place on that February night, 2012? Did I speak the truth, nothing but the truth? Only God and the accused know what really took place on that February night.

RISING FROM THE ASHES

What I see emerging like a phoenix from the ashes is that law makers are beginning to see that America will never realize her true potential, if there is no justice in the law… if the system is broken. They have begun to see the writing on the wall: united we stand, divided we crumble.

Unless the laws which are presently on the books, which say: one sets of laws for blacks and the other sets of laws for whites.. get thrown into a lake of fire; racial and social injustices will continue, so will poverty and crime. and finally, the country will die a slow death.

Who will come to her rescue… these great United States of America? tell me! who will come to her rescue? Does she (America) have any friends left out there?

Please allow me to conclude this book with a poem and an excerpt, titled: The Meaning of the name Mandela to me, from my book:

MY FAVORITE POEMS

TREAT YOUR FRIENDS WITH RESPECT

Boast not in wisdom or in the strength of your arms because they shall fail.

Let not pride break your sail.

Treat your friends with respect.

Repeat their names in your speeches and their efforts, do bring to light.

Esteem them highly in your chambers; less they forget you in the days of your troubles, when terror knocks on your door, in the middle of the night.

The meaning of the name MANDELA to me.

M: is for mission, a duty he did so very well; for that very purpose was he born, I can tell. Oh yes; there are many who wondered how was it possible that he could have accomplished so much in so little time, after his release from jail. May I dare say; he walked a thin line.

The roads he travelled to reach his destination were never paved, never smooth. They were rough roads with sharp stones and thorns on either side. There were many hills, steep hills and many valleys, deep, deep valleys but he didn't quit. He looked far ahead and saw the prize and pressed forward with courage.

He had reasons to be bitter, bitter against a system that continually preached hate, violence and death against a defenseless people... a vulnerable people.

He had reason to be bitter against the system that did not want prosperity for the black and brown people of South Africa.

Three hundred years of suppression… the beatings and the killing of his people? Oh yes; he had reasons to be bitter, and to be hostile and to seek revenge but he didn't seek revenge. He won freedom for his people and all South Africans who were under the bondage of Apartheid. He could have quit because the roads were rough and the hills were steep and the valleys were deep and dark and cold, oh yes! but he looked ahead, far… ahead and saw a speck of light and so he pressed forward with courage; that's who he was!

A: is for Aspiration. He sought out justice and peace through humility. He was bold and wise.

He looked evil in the eye and said, get thee behind me Satan.

He had courage and it sustained him.

He aspired towards greatness and it discovered him.

He turned the other cheek and the world applauded. People of great stature were astounded. Is that the man who was left to die in dungeon deep, dark and cold, they asked? Is that the same man who fought 'long-side his people for basic human rights who was met with dogs, man-eating dogs, bullets and the full force of injustice? That was their plight but he pressed forward boldly and brought his people out of darkness into a marvelous light.

Madiba, Madiba, shouted the people, people from around the Globe.

His was loved and is loved; I see it and I know it. His presence is felt from shore to shore. His humility and courage is forever embedded on the human psyche and for that, the world is a better place.

Rest on my fearless friend, rest on.

N: is for nurturing. He cared for the development of his people, not just people of color but people of all races. He believed that there is strength in unity and so he pressed forward with courage and won the people's hearts, black and white. He was their leader. They called him Father of a free society… father of their new world. We are witnesses to his courage which unveiled to man that out of many, we can be one people.

There was a void, and he stepped in and filled it:
a void for teaching fairness, honesty and truth,
a void in oneness and wholesomeness towards the poor and people of color..

Where there was weakness; he stepped in and showed strength.

He steadied the hands of the feeble and gave them hope.

He led them through the deep Seas and not one of them was lost.

He was their Moses, a modern day Moses. He was real.

His love for peace and passion for justice for all people has touched the hearts of many around the world. He was loved and will always be loved for his nurturing spirit.

D: is for dad. He was a fearless dad, a wise dad, unselfish and kind. He sacrificed his own family to rescue other families from the evil grip of unjust laws – Apartheid. He moved forward with courage and boldness, even when there was weakness and skepticism within his rank and those around him; he moved forward and never looked backward, into the darkness of hate and instability.

He realized his purpose on earth and understood that there was such little time to accomplish all that which had to be done to bring hope and prosperity to his country – a country that was built on fear and hate.

Positive change will come one day, he said, in not so many words, it's not going to be easy but it will come. He looked to his left and to his right and on either side there were deep, deep waters but he looked ahead again and saw a speck of light; he then took up his mantle of love, peace, hope, prosperity and all that is good and moved forward with courage.

He built schools and playgrounds for his children. He built new roads and houses in the villages and those that lived within were in awe, they never believed that in there life-time, such prosperity would have been realized

He fed the young and the old alike with good foods. And the dried bones in the valleys became alive again and flesh was added to them and their beauty begun to shine like wild flowers on top of the hillsides round about.

And so we see, Madiba, the great spirit, the spirit of boldness and courage must step into his whirlwind and like Elijah; his Mantle is left behind not just for South Africans but for the entire world.

E: is for Elder. He was an Elder to his people, a leader…a good leader, a States man, a revolutionist, whose aspirations were for change and he could not be denied...

Change to unjust laws, change to the hearts and minds of a people who could not see past their own self-righteousness.

The task that was at hand looked impossible to be approached much less to be taken on, but if I perish, I perish, said Madiba, freedom shall be won. Yes, he did continue to press forward with courage and boldness.

And so he took his people on a journey; it was a rocky journey. It was a journey filled with troubles and trials. There were much grumblings and uneasiness, doubters and those who would have liked to take a step back into the darkness, into the evil hands of poverty and confusion but Madiba stood up with boldness and courage and declared to the people that CHANGE would not be easy. Change would take much time to be realized. Prosperity does not come overnight; that's what I heard from that great voice.

TRAYVON B. MARTIN

He did not just speak about oneness and love to his country men and women, boys and girls... he spoke to the whole world, that without UNITY, prosperity will never be realized in any nation, and he revealed clearly for all to see that the security of a nation depends on the unity of its people.

L: is for Leader, a good leader, he knew when to speak and when to hold his tongue. He was a fearless leader who would break down iron fences to win freedom and a sense of hope for his people through peaceful means.

Madiba, the father of a democratic South Africa; led his people to a new and exciting height, not seen by any generation since Moses led the children of Israel from the land of the Egyptians into a new world.

He showed love, impartial love to all his fellow citizens. He had a big heart. He had clarity of thinking. He never once looked at the white people and said, now is the time for retribution because, he never lost sight of the mission. He called his people together, black and white, then said he, in words and in actions, come now! it's time for us to unite as one.

He was the type of leader who had a great sense of timing. He knew when to step aside… when to pass the mantle on. There is a new generation of leaders to come. Let them continue the work, he must have thought..

    No more standing on the sideline. Step in and do what must be done. Be the leader of the next generation if that is what you were called to do. Lead and be a good leader and others will follow. That is what I heard from that beautiful soul -of –a- man and leader:

Nelson Mandela.

A: is for achievements. No other human being, in modern history has ever achieved so much in such short span of time. Not only was he a moral champion but he was also a political giant.

His first 25 years; a young Mandela saw a LONG WALK TO FREEDOM but he was not afraid to move forward with courage on behalf of his people who had no quality of life, no justice in basic human rights; they needed a voice and he gave his.

He lost his freedom, in his struggle for justice. He spent 27 years in a dark and lonely cell; sick and weak at times but he never gave up; he was always looking ahead even from that lonely place.

Even though he was isolated from his people and the world, he was still their strength, and their hope because they knew that he was on a mission that would bring them into prosperity and oneness.

From a jail cell, to becoming the country's first democratic leader without a shot been fired was astounding not just for the people of South Africa but for many people around the world.

Some called him a radical, others, a terrorist, but that never dithered him from the mission. He knew where he was going and what he had to do to get there. And he knew that the enemies of peace, love and prosperity would one day see the light.

Many blessings be upon the Mandela family. They have sacrificed much in giving of their beloved Nelson Mandela to their country and the world. He was the one that showed his country and the world that wars can be fought and won without one shot being fired. He brought the enemies of justice and equality together and the world saw how the two worked alongside each other to bring about unity.

Prosperity can only now be realized with time, unity and patience. Press forward with courage as did your dear leader; people of South Africa, and please send that same message to all the leaders of nations, around the Globe.

THE MISSION: Love not Hate, Peace not War. Equality for all, that is the formula for success, not just for South Africans but for all people, rich or poor.

Rest in peace great friend. Your life's work lives on.

Copyright © L. Pryce, 2013

All rights reserved. No part of this book may be Reproduced in any form or by any Electronic or Mechanical means, including information Storage and Retrieval systems without permission in writing from the publisher, except by a publisher, who quotes brief passages in a review.

LEONS PUBLISHING

Leepry023@gmail.com

leepry023@gmail.com

416 477 0831

Also by the same Author:

1. CEREBRAL SUM --- A PUZZLE BOOK

ISBN: 9781490363639

2. MY FAVORITE POEMS ---POETRY BOOK

ISBN: 9780968196403

3. AWESOME GOD---understanding the Godhead --Unpublished

4. Boom-a-Rang ---THE Proffessor who created the perfect bullet deflector is being sought by the KGB – Unpublished

Please get them on Amazon.com, type in the name of the book of you choice and the full name of the author or the ISBN number.

All rights reserved
Copyright © 2013 L. Pryce

Sources:
Public records and live courtroom dramas

www.ingramcontent.com/pod-product-compliance
Lightning Source LLC
Chambersburg PA
CBHW042309150426
43198CB00001B/20